CRABTREE CONTACT

PARKOUR

Dan Edwardes

 Crabtree Publishing Company

www.crabtreebooks.com

Crabtree Publishing Company

www.crabtreebooks.com   1-800-387-7650
Copyright © **2009 CRABTREE PUBLISHING COMPANY**.

**Published
in Canada
Crabtree Publishing**
616 Welland Ave.
St. Catharines, ON
L2M 5V6

**Published in the
United States
Crabtree Publishing**
PMB 59051
350 Fifth Ave., 59th Floor
New York, NY 10118

Author: Dan Edwardes
Project editor: Ruth Owen
Project designer: Simon Fenn
Photo research: Ruth Owen
Project coordinator: Robert Walker
Production coordinator: Katherine Berti
Prepress technicians: Samara Parent
    Katherine Berti, Ken Wright

Thank you to
Lorraine Petersen
and the members
of nasen

Content development by Shakespeare Squared
www.ShakespeareSquared.com

Picture credits:
Big Pictures: p. 23
Corbis: Gareth Brown: front cover
Andy Day: p. 1, 4, 5, 6, 7 (right), 8, 9, 10, 11 (top),
    11 (bottom), 12–13, 14, 15, 17, 18, 19, 20, 22, 24,
    25, 28–29
Paul Holmes: p. 31 (both)
Parkour Generations: p. 7 (left), 7 (center)
Shutterstock: p. 2–3, 7 (background), 8–9 (background),
    10–11 (background), 16 (background), 19 (background),
    21, 23 (background), 26–27

Every effort has been made to trace copyright holders, and we apologize in
advance for any omissions. We would be pleased to insert the appropriate
acknowledgments in any subsequent edition of this publication.

Library and Archives Canada Cataloguing in Publication

Edwardes, Dan
    Parkour / Dan Edwardes.

(Crabtree contact)
Includes index.
ISBN 978-0-7787-3821-3 (bound).--ISBN 978-0-7787-3842-8 (pbk.)

    1. Extreme sports--Juvenile literature.   2. Parkour--Juvenile
literature. I. Title. II. Series: Crabtree contact

GV749.7.E38 2009   j796.04'6   C2008-907864-0

Printed in Canada/012013/DM20121114

Library of Congress Cataloging-in-Publication Data

Edwardes, Dan.
    Parkour / Dan Edwardes.
       p. cm. -- (Crabtree contact)
    Includes index.
    ISBN 978-0-7787-3842-8 (pbk. : alk. paper) -- ISBN
978-0-7787-3821-3 (reinforced library binding : alk. paper)
    1. Extreme sports--Juvenile literature. 2. Parkour--Juvenile
literature. I. Title. II. Series.

    GV749.7.E385 2009
    796.04'6--dc22

                                                    2008052408

CONTENTS

Chapter 1
Parkour! 4

Chapter 2
History of Parkour 6

Chapter 3
Training........................8

Chapter 4
Parkour Techniques.............12

Chapter 5
Mental Challenge...............20

Chapter 6
In the Public Eye...............22

Chapter 7
Parkour Vision..................26

Chapter 8
A Way of Life 28

Need-to-know Words..........30

Learning Parkour/
Parkour Online 31

Index.....................32

WARNING!

CHAPTER 1

PARKOUR!

Dynamic.

Explosive.

Powerful.

Precise.

This is parkour!

Moving through the city.
Running and leaping.
Overcoming any **obstacle** in your path.
Never stopping. Always moving.

Parkour is a new and exciting activity. The aim of
parkour is to move around an area, such as a city or
park, without stopping. People who take part in parkour
run, climb, and jump over buildings and obstacles.

CHAPTER 2

HISTORY OF PARKOUR

Parkour was created by a group of young men in France in the 1980s and 1990s.

Parkour's first name was *Art du Deplacement*. In English, this means the "Art of Displacement."

Displacement means getting from one place to another using only your own body.

The name later changed to "parkour."
In England, parkour was also called "freerunning."

The **founders** of parkour called their group "Yamakasi."

Three of the Yamakasi founders

Yann Hnautra

Laurent Piemontesi

Chau Belle-Dinh

Yamakasi is a word from the Lingala language in Africa. It means "strong man, strong spirit."

The group's goal was to become fit, strong, and fast.

The founders wanted to become people who could meet any challenge.

CHAPTER 3 TRAINING

Parkour is very difficult. It requires a lot of training to be able to **practice** safely and correctly.

*A parkour instructor teaches a group some basic **vaults***

The best way to learn is to be taught by experienced instructors.

Parkour is a way of mastering your own movement.
It is a way of training your body to achieve its
full **potential**.

You can do much more than you think.
Your body and mind can do amazing things
when properly trained.

Training is hard, but always good fun!

Parkour is about physical fitness and functional strength.

Functional strength means being able to move your body wherever you want to go. This includes being able to climb, run, jump, drop, and twist.

You need to prepare your muscles and bones for these movements. This is known as "conditioning."

The best way to condition your body is to repeat natural, functional movements in the places you are going to practice in.

Parkour also requires regular physical training such as bodyweight drills.

A bodyweight drill is an exercise that develops your muscles. The exercise uses only the weight of your body, not solid weights.

You must improve your jump strength.

You must also improve your ability to absorb **impact** when you land.

CHAPTER 4

PARKOUR TECHNIQUES

There are as many different ways to move in parkour as there are people who practice it!

JUMPS

Parkour has many different types of jumps to learn. These include running jumps, standing jumps, drops, and **precision** jumps.

Practitioners of parkour spend long hours practicing how to take off and land well.

They train their legs to absorb the impact of the jump safely and in a controlled way.

Experienced practitioners can make very precise jumps of up to 19 feet (6 m) in length.

Precision jumping practice is very important in parkour. You must be able to land in perfect balance on thin or small objects such as railings or walls.

VAULTS

A vault is a movement that allows you to move over an obstacle and keep moving.

A vault is normally used for obstacles that are at chest height.

Most vaults involve jumping over an obstacle while placing the hands on it for control and direction.

The *Saut de Chat* is one type of vault.
It means the "jump of the cat." It is a good
way to move over low obstacles quickly.

Practitioners dive headfirst over an obstacle.
They place both hands on the obstacle.
Then they bring their knees through their arms.

WALL-RUNNING

A wall-run is a way to get over a very high obstacle or wall.

Practitioners run at a wall.

They place a foot on the wall at about waist height.

Then they push up while reaching with their arms.

A good wall-run can help practitioners reach the top of a wall that is up to 16 feet (5 m) high.

Wall-runs are very explosive movements!

ARM JUMPS

Jumping and grabbing onto an edge, such as the top of a wall, is known as a *Saut de Bras* in French. It means "arm jump" in English.

This move is also known as a "cat leap."

An arm jump is used when a wall or obstacle is too high to jump onto directly.

You must grab the top of the wall with your arms and then pull yourself up.

Arm jumps require a lot of upper body strength.

You can cover huge distances between obstacles using an arm jump.

Training for parkour takes time, so please don't rush. There are no short cuts and no secrets—just **discipline**.

CHAPTER 3

MENTAL CHALLENGE

Parkour is far more than just a physical discipline. Parkour challenges the mind in many ways.

You must learn to overcome your fear and inhibitions about movement.

An inhibition is a feeling that stops you from doing something.

You must master your thoughts and learn
to focus your attention.

Parkour builds confidence and inner control.

Parkour helps you control your body
and thoughts.

CHAPTER 6

IN THE PUBLIC EYE

In 1997 there was a movie made called *Yamakasi*. It starred the French founders of parkour.

In the movie, the Yamakasi use their amazing skills to raise money for a young boy who needs an operation.

The movie was filmed in Paris. It showed how parkour can be used to get around a city very fast.

Then, in 2003, a British **documentary** was released called *Jump London*.

The documentary was filmed all over London. It showed some of London's most impressive buildings and famous places.

Practicing parkour in London

After *Jump London* was released, parkour became huge around the world.

Now, parkour appears in major Hollywood movies.

Casino Royale

Parkour was used in the opening scene of the James Bond movie *Casino Royale*.

James Bond chases a villain through a city and across roofs and cranes. It was an explosive opening to the movie!

REMEMBER

The incredible moves you see in movies, magazines, and books are performed by trained professionals.

Parkour is a stunning visual art. It has been featured in music videos and magazine and TV advertisements.

Parkour has been used to advertise clothes, phones, and cars.

A New York photoshoot for clothing company, Ecko.

This photograph is from a photoshoot for a German magazine. Parkour practitioners showed off their moves while wearing clothes from top designers.

Fashion companies always like to show off their designs in a dynamic way!

CHAPTER 7

PARKOUR VISION

Practicing parkour will change your way of seeing the buildings and area around you.

You begin to see new ways of moving through a city or a park.

You see new ways of using the buildings and objects around you.

Your **vision** changes completely!

CHAPTER 8 | A WAY OF LIFE

For those who practice parkour, it becomes more than just a pastime or a hobby.

It changes the way they think about themselves and the place where they live.

Parkour helps practitioners improve in every way.

Parkour becomes a way of life for its practitioners. They learn that they can overcome problems in their lives—not only in training!

NEED-TO-KNOW WORDS

discipline The ability to commit to practicing and training regularly and with focus

documentary A factual TV show or movie

founder A person who starts something, such as an organization or a sport

impact The force that goes through your body when you land from a jump

obstacle A wall, park bench, set of steps—anything you can move over when practicing parkour

potential What your mind and body are capable of if you train hard

practice This word can be used in two ways. It can mean when a person takes part in an activity. It can also mean doing something again and again to improve

practitioner A person who practices (takes part) in an activity

precision Being very accurate with your movements and landings from jumps

technique A way of doing something

vault A movement that allows you to move over an obstacle and keep moving

vision The ability to see new possibilities for movement in your surroundings

LEARNING PARKOUR

If you want to practice parkour, it is best to learn from a qualified teacher or an experienced practitioner.

- For help on joining classes, go to www.parkourgenerations.com You will find information on groups and classes in your community.

- All you need to take part are running shoes and simple training clothes such as sportswear—nothing else!

- Classes always involve tough physical training and a lot of practice of the movements of parkour. It can be hard work!

Dan Edwardes teaches a parkour class

PARKOUR ONLINE

www.parkourgenerations.com./
Information about parkour and where to find classes

www.majesticforce.com/
More great parkour information

www.kiell.com/
Great parkour photographs

Publisher's note to educators and parents:
Our editors have carefully reviewed these websites to ensure that they are suitable for children. Many websites change frequently, however, and we cannot guarantee that a site's future contents will continue to meet our high standards of quality and educational value. Be advised that children should be closely supervised whenever they access the Internet.

INDEX

A
advertisements 24–25
arm jumps 18–19
Art du Deplacement 6
Art of Displacement 6

B
Belle-Dinh, Chau 7
bodyweight drills 11
Bond, James 23

C
Casino Royale 23
cat leap 18
classes in parkour 8, 31
conditioning 10

E
Edwardes, Dan 7, 31

F
fears (overcoming) 20
founders of parkour 7, 22
freerunning 7
functional strength 10

H
history of parkour 6–7
Hnautra, Yann 7

I
inhibitions (overcoming) 20

J
Jump London 22–23
jump of the cat 15
jumps 11, 12–13

L
Lingala language 7

M
mental challenge 20–21
movies 22–23
music videos 24

O
obstacles 26–27, 30

P
Piemontesi, Laurent 7
potential of your body 5, 9
potential of your mind 5, 9,
   20–21
precision jumps 13

S
safety issues 8, 23
Saut de Bras 18–19
Saut de Chat 15

T
techniques 12–13, 14–15,
   16–17, 18–19
training 8–9, 10–11, 19, 31

V
vaults 14–15

W
wall-runs 16–17

Y
Yamakasi (group) 7
Yamakasi (movie) 22